Das Wird Sich Alles Finden
[everything will turn out alright]

Arts Collinwood
Cleveland, OH, USA
April 5-27, 2013

Bloc Projects
Sheffield, UK
December 7-21, 2012

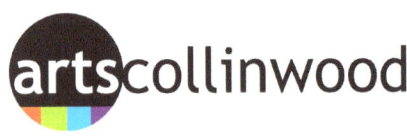

Acknowledgements

I would like to thank all of the artists participating in Das Wird Sich Alles Finden. After the satisfaction of being chosen for an international exhibit in 2011, the artists were subsequently abandoned by the organizer of the exhibit and left without a show. Instead of resigning to misfortune and succumbing to resentment, they began communicating amongst themselves and used the obstacle as a catalyst for collaboration; creating a new fate for the show. It is appropriate that Arts Collinwood would host such an exhibit, as it harkens back to the origins of the gallery and the many artists who came together more than ten years ago to overcome the obstacles of the Collinwood neighborhood and create a space where serious artistic endeavors could be shared with the community. True of this exhibit, as is often true in life, the faith that 'Everything Will Turn Out All Right' determined a favorable outcome. It has been through the faith of many artists and volunteers who believed that North Collinwood could be a neighborhood with a great quality of life, with cultural institutions, parks, libraries and great entertainment, that have brought about the positive changes we are seeing today.

Arts Collinwood is fortunate to be a small and nimble organization, which can take advantage when serendipity presents an opportunity such as this one. I would like to thank Mark Keffer, who volunteers on our gallery committee and is one of the artists in Das Wird Sich Alles Finden, for advocating that the exhibit show in our gallery and for asking Christopher L. Richards to curate the project.

And finally, I would like to extend a very special note of appreciation to Christopher L. Richards for the many hours he spent volunteering to make this show a reality. As curator of the exhibition, Christopher liaised with all the artists, negotiated the logistics, from shipping to installation and, designed and produced the catalog. Quite simply, Das Wird Alles Finden would not have happened without Christopher's hard work and Arts Collinwood is deeply grateful for his dedication to the project.

Amy Callahan, Director

Das Wird Sich Alles Finden
[everything will turn out alright]

In 2011, a group of international artists applied for an exhibit in Berlin called Hasenheide. The exhibit was to present contemporary paintings, prints and drawings, but fell short of describing any further aim in its thesis. The organizer of the show chose from its applicants and contacted the artists to inform them of their inclusion. Even a website was developed and posted, announcing the exhibit and listing the participating artists. Soon after however, the curator disappeared. Emails and phone calls remained unanswered, refunds of the application fee were not issued. No explanation as to the progress, or lack thereof, was published. Until early 2013, the website remained live.

Many of the artists felt anger and rejection. Most were left confused and dismayed. Correspondence between the artists started the development of an idea: to exhibit together and not be made into victims. While the original Berlin exhibit would not happen, other exhibits could. Those artists interested in making the most out of a bad experience decided to work together. Reflecting on the experience and having a sense of hope from a shattered promise, they wanted the exhibit to instill the feeling of coming up out of a dark place and reaching for a positive ending. In a tongue-in-cheek stab at the event that brought them together the artists chose a German title, Das Wird Sich Alles Finden, which appropriately translates to, "everything will turn out all right."

At first glance, the work of these artists is very diverse and seemingly unconnected. Through different mediums and styles, some work appears wild and vibrant, controlled and exacting, or minimal and somber. Yet all of these artists have key elements which bring what could be a disjointed body of work into a cohesive whole. The focus of the exhibit became personal identity in the surrounding environment and the use of language, verbal and visual, in which it is defined. The explorations of linear time through overlapping messages, the confusing bombardment of information pair with ego driven fiction, absurd narratives and standoffish portraiture gives us a glimpse of how we respond to the world around us. Fading memories and confusing abstractions with possible representational imagery tell us that the perception of our surroundings may not always be what we think they are, while made up written languages and primitive marks explore the drive to document our human experiences and define ourselves as creative beings.

As those creative beings, much of our identity is based in our own minds. As Joshua Thomson explores a humorous critique of the status in which many artists perceive themselves. Through film and stop motion animation, he questions notions of artistic genius. Thomas takes on the concepts of truth and memory through the creation of his own personal histories and presents a parody of himself that acts also as a fictitious fulfillment of his own artistic ambitions. This presentation of an interior world thrust outward onto others shows how our projection of self can be completely off base from how those around us view our identity.

The portraiture of Lydia Panas furthers the concept of identity from within, but also allows for the influence of the artist and viewer to take part in creating the persona. Panas' work captures the insecurities and expectations of her sitters, who allow for a level of intimacy that is paradoxical. Are these people presenting themselves openly, or are they ultimately guarded? The vagueness sheds light on the internal and external struggle to define who we are, and how we interact with the world around us.

Intimacy as a means of communicating the concept of self is a course that Yoonsuk Choi employs in a diptych video that presents the artist in a daily ritual of cleaning a bed and the contents of the lint roller used as evidence of a person's presence. The trivial repetitious aspects of life translates into a poetic drawing consisting of both the span of time spent performing a mundane task that often falls from memory and the collection of hair, lint and dirt which creates a visual record of what has passed. Time and debris allocate a concept of self in the physical world, often ignored, which we can all identify with.

Forgotten moments pervade the photography of Amandine Crozate. Her work blends the real world with that of the imagination. Her series, Instants volés, or stolen moments, creates the fog of a memory or a feeling that is fleeting and not quite complete. Void of the human figure, the images allude to a personal presence but it is ambiguous and otherworldly. This questions just how much of ourselves is lost as our memories fade? Similar lost memories are at the core of Krystel Marois' photographs. Invoking emotion through human presence and absence, Marois conjures the temporal experience of the human experience. This type of portraiture allows the sitter to be singular in their thoughts, while permitting the viewer to read the work through what is presented in the image, and through their own inner narrative. A satirical take on narrative, Niall Dooley's comic-like style creates a humorous narrative in which he examines the human condition. Often, his scenarios depict a paradoxical aspect of societal issues and how an individual might react to them.

Combining photography with fabric, embroidery and crochet, Patricia Casey delves into the mystery of day dreams and recollections. Inspired by Janet Frame's novel, Scented Gardens for the Blind, Casey explores the mind's secret interior worlds. Her work, while primarily photography based, combines craft and mixed media techniques to further place her work in a netherworld of the imagination. Similarly, Mark Keffer's work teeters on the edges of consciousness initiating a language that is devoid of the verbal and is instead geared to the visual as much as possible. Through abstractions, he utilizes both organic and hard edged structures atop a hazy void allowing for the viewer to determine the meaning through their own sense of self.

This questioning of the cognitive process in relation to our vision of the self and our surroundings continues in the work of Margaret Withers. In an ever evolving conversation with the viewer, Withers presents an abstract form between non-objective images, and something slightly recognizable. It is a collaboration between the artist and the viewer, as well as other viewers. One might see a meaning in the paintings that changes the concepts of another's interpretation. In turn, additional viewings may bring out an even deeper personal understanding, or even contradict the viewer's initial response all together. Kayde Anobile challenges these paradoxes along with the uncanny. She often presents multiples, and conflicting images to question identity and the cognitive process. Overlapping monochromatic drawings present a situation of confusion between flat and perspective space.

The proliferation of overlapping stimuli in contemporary communications and how we comprehend it compels the work of Jonathan McFadden. The notion of understanding – or lack of understanding – in a landscape of constantly changing cycles of media information, McFadden uses digital imagery and geographical information to create a decorative pattern that expresses the fast paced jumble of messages that bombard us in our everyday lives. He sees this global trend as promoting a lack of memory and attempts to dramatize its effects through his densely layered imagery. Similarly, Julia Schmid embraces how our thinking and communication is effected by collective knowledge. Developed from the rapidly and steadily increasing flow of information, she questions how much we really know versus how much we pretend to know. Quick repetitive marks create a kind of pattern that remains unintelligible.

More traditional print media is embraced by Lesley Guy as she questions the value of identity posthumous. Collecting and archiving obituaries, she became fascinated with how the entirety of a person's life was reduced to a photograph and a few paragraphs. While the histories of the people in the works have meaning, it is only on a superficial level. More important is the composition of the layout and how it informs the drawing. She instead plays with the surface and the picture plane, allowing form to deface the biography of the deceased.

Robert Lang also questions the purpose of traditional media communications. Lang uses painting to understand his relationship with his decisions pertaining to a perceived reality and everyday experiences. Through an abstract economy of paint strokes and thinly glazed layers across the cover of a book, he negates any purposeful function allowing for the viewer to discover their own interpretations based on their individual or cultural backgrounds.

However, written language is embraced by Mercedes Teixido and Haroob Mullick. Teixido takes inspiration from poetry and signage. Seeing drawing as language, she views these drawings as "being performed into existence." They become an invented alphabet forming a sentence of images. The dialogue is thus reinvented as a cultural activity. Mullick reaches into the distant past with primitive marks. Working from a formula, Haroob Mullick creates a flowing personal narrative that straddles constraint and freedom in the manner in which he makes a mark. The endeavor of creating these marks is then turned over to the relationship between the subconscious and the materials being used.

Ultimately, these types of communication are expressive of our self to the outer world. One which we are forced to individually comprehend in an ever competing conglomerate of information imposing itself upon us. These artists examine our contemporary situation and how we define both ourselves and the world in it. Though the intent of the initial curator may not have been to examine these themes, the selected works lend themselves to a deeper and interconnected reading of a struggle to define the self and it's place in a truly global society.

Christopher L. Richards, Curator

Kayde Anobile

Patricia Casey

Yoonsuk Choi

Amandine Crozat

Niall Dooley

Lesley Guy

Mark Keffer

Robert Lang

Krystel Marois

Jonathan McFadden

Haroob Mullick

Lydia Panas

Julia Schmid

Mercedes Teixido

Joshua Thomson

Margaret Withers

Kayde Anobile

Istanbul, Turkey

STATEMENT:

Kayde Anobile is interested in paradoxical outcomes and in the cognitive dissonance caused by presenting contradictory ideas simultaneously. The uncanny space created where opposing ideas overlap is where she situates her work.

ABOUT:

Kayde Anobile is currently represented by Tintype gallery, London, and has work in the Zabludowicz collection. She received a BFA from SAIC (the school of the art institute of Chicago) and an MA from Chelsea College of Art and Design in London. She currently lives and works in Istanbul.

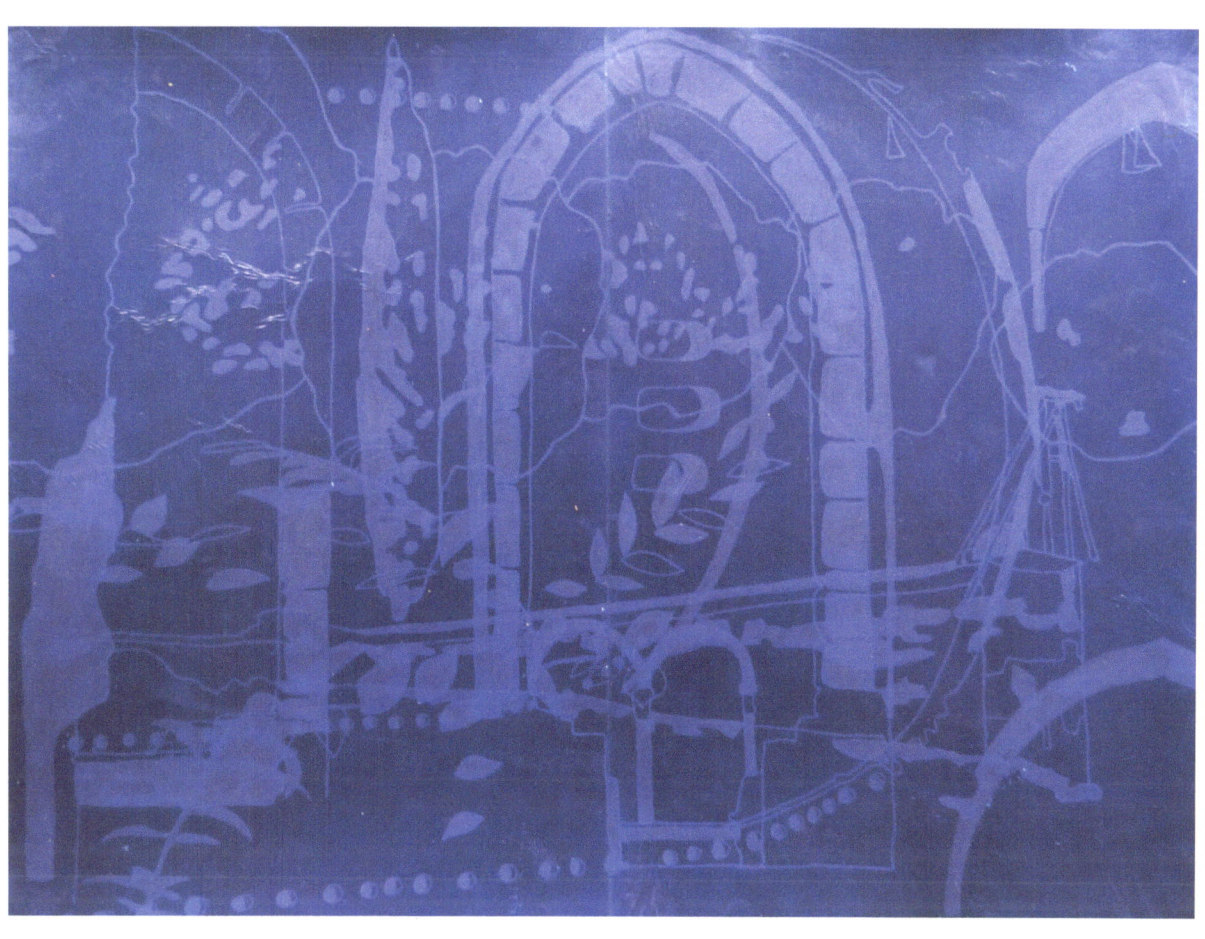

Untitled, 2012
Blue carbon paper on wood panel
40cm x 29cm

* This piece is on consignment from Tintype gallery, London

Patricia Casey

Sydney, Australia

ABOUT:

Winner of the HeadOn Photographic Portrait Prize in 2006, Patricia Casey has been a practicing artist since 1999 and has exhibited in group and solo exhibitions during this time. She completed her Master of Visual Arts (Research) degree in 2009 and Master of Studio Arts in 2006 at the University of Sydney. Patricia was a finalist in the National Photography Prize in 2010 and also in the Sir John Sulman Prize at the Art Gallery of NSW in 2002 and 2005. In 2002 she was also selected for the public art exhibition, "Sydney Looking Forward" as part of Art and About. She has received a number of awards and her work has been exhibited overseas in China, Korea, France, Malaysia and America. Patricia's work has also been shown, in regional and interstate galleries, including the Queensland Centre for Photography in 2009, 2010, 2012 and at the Perth Centre for Photography in 2012. Her work is represented in a number of prestigious collections, including Macquarie Bank, Frasers Property Group and the Gutman collection. Patricia is represented by NG Art in Sydney and her eighth solo exhibition Elsewhere was held in February, 2012.

Imagine None of this is Real, 2012
Photography, Metallic Threads,
Crochet Cotton Lace, Pins
Dimensions variable

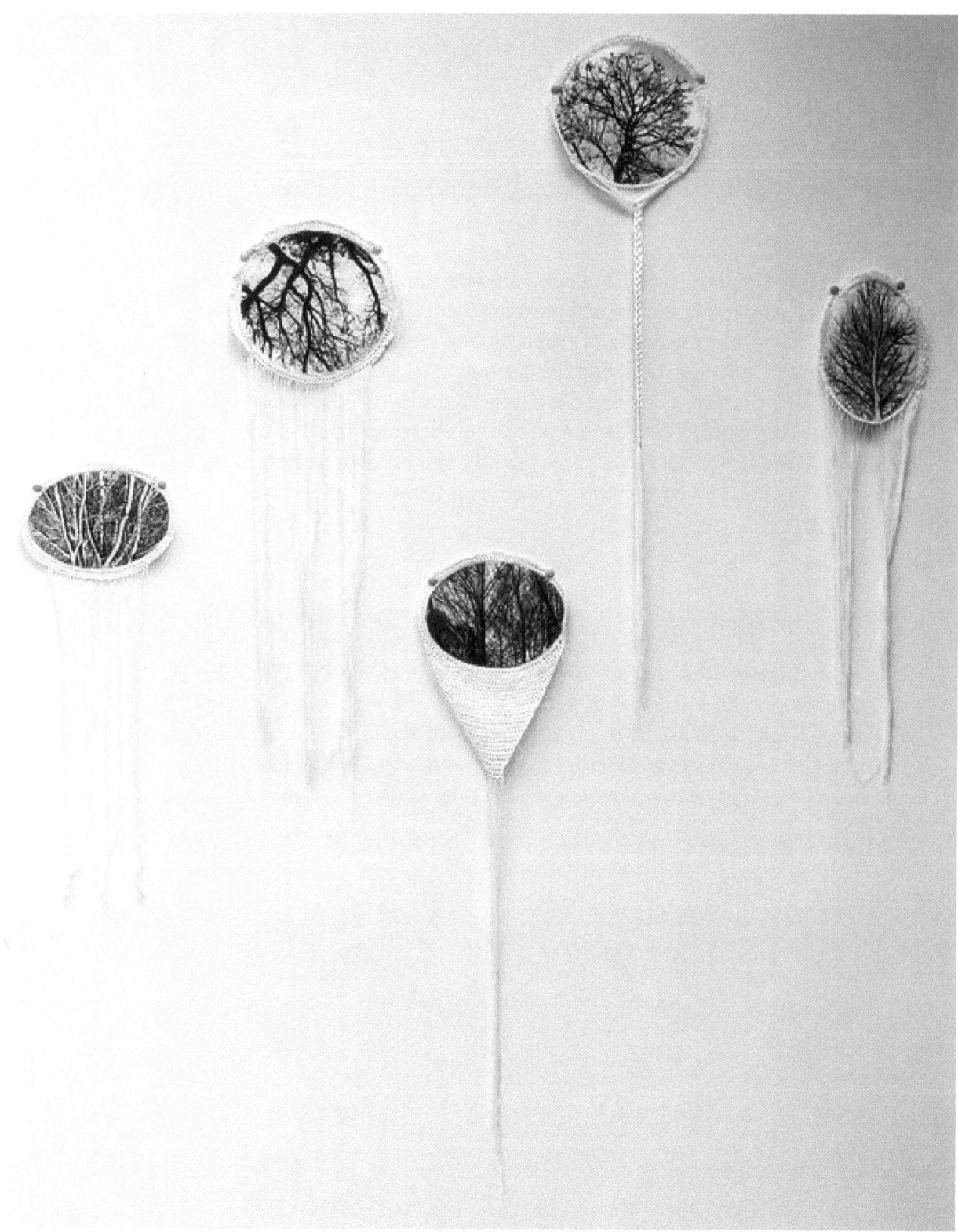

Yoonsuk Choi

London, England

STATEMENT:

I am interested in discovering and collecting the ambiguous visuals which is caused by perpetual routines and personal habits. It is originated from my curiosity towards the origin of inspiration of an artist. By having that, I observe myself and allow utilising the surroundings; daily objects, physical limitation of human body and the notion of time. My intention is to explore the engagement between art and artist's personal life and trying to resolve and manifest it in visual language. My subjects often relate to the nature of drawing, and try to share its tactile and acoustic experience.

ABOUT:

Yoonsuk Choi received a BFA in painting from Chung-Any University in Seoul, Korea, and an MFA in painting from The Slade School of Fine Art, University College London, London, UK. Choi's work has been included in a number of exhibitions including *The Power of Young Artists*, Bunam Gallery in Seoul in 2006, *Art in Focus: Black and White Flower Painting*, Imperial College Healthcare Charity Art Committee in London in 2010, and *The Traces: Collective Surroundings*, Hanmi Gallery in London in 2011.

Still from: *Bed Scene*, 2012
Single channel video
2'00"

Amandine Crozat

Paris, France

STATEMENT:

Stolen Moments plunges us into a ghostly place, haunted by the presence of clothes in full flight. A feeling of solitude and weightlessness dominates these mysterious scenes which are at once poetic and enigmatic. Between invisible presence and visible absence, the viewer is invited to view a scene to which only he appears to be the witness. Is this an impression given by the wind, or is this the result of a ghostly apparition?

ABOUT:

Graduated with a Masters Degree in Plastic Arts from the University of Paris I, Amandine Crozat lives and works in Paris. Being inspired by her many travels and using photography as well as installation to make her phantasmagoric scenographies, she has participated in many collective exhibitions since 2007, especially the 53rd Salon d'Art Contemporain de Montrouge, Autour des RIP d'Arles (Festival International de l'Image Environnementale), Hidden Sense - 2010 International Exhibition for Young Photographers (special event of Daegu Photo Biennale 2010) and also in an international residency COMP (Crossing of Movements Project) in South Korea finalized by a showcase in the island of Jeju in November 2010. She has been finalist of Make History Second Edition Exhibition in Modena, Italy and has recently exhibited in Berlin, then in Paris for the Rencontres Photographiques du 10ème.

Left:
Instants volés #1 (Stolen moments), 2010
C-print, 40 x 60 cm

Right:
Instants volés #2 (Stolen moments), 2010
C-print, 60 x 90 cm

Bottom:
Instants volés #3 (Stolen moments), 2010
C-print, 60 x 90 cm

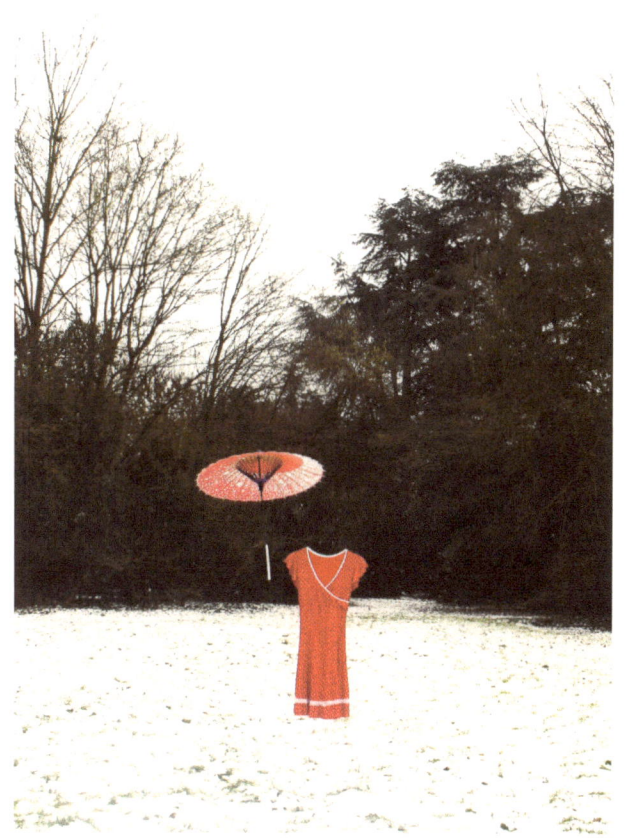
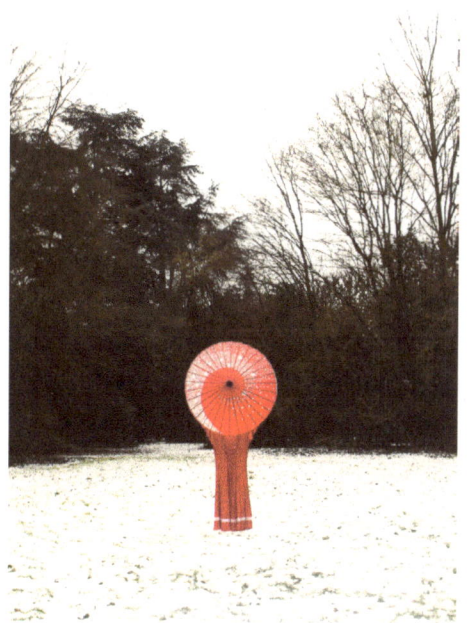
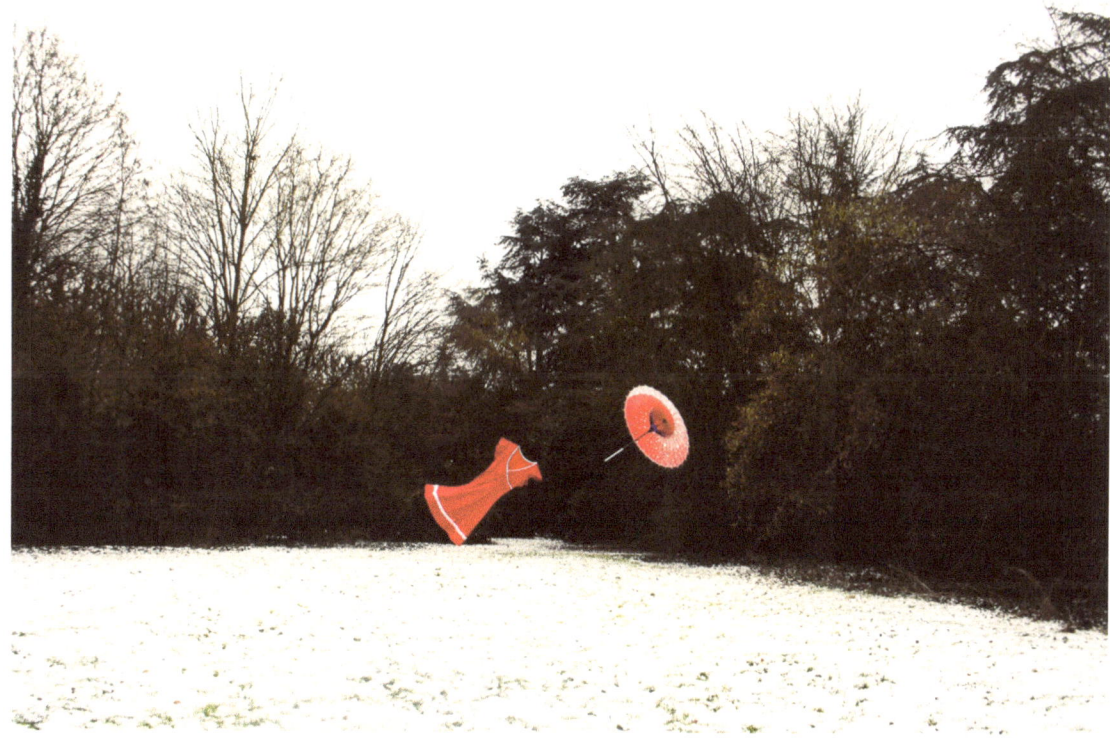

Niall Dooley

Dublin, Ireland

Dublin, Ireland

STATEMENT:

Niall Dooley makes drawings of people in ordered and purposeful scenarios. Through a comic like drawing style he employs the use of symbols and the arrangement of figures in a particular order to set up intriguing and humorous scenarios which highlight the paradoxical aspects of human involvement.

Dooley's drawings depict often surreal settings creating narratives and visual metaphors which can refer to probing issues about society and the human condition, They can also be purely playful reveling in the idea of paradox and the absurd as a means to communicate feeling images.

ABOUT:

Niall Dooley is an Irish visual artist who graduated in 2009 with a Honours Bachelors Degree in fine art painting at NCAD. He has been living and working in Dublin since his graduation.

Top:
Bilateral Attraction, 2010
pencil pen and acyrlic on paper
8 x 11.75 inches

Bottom Left:
As Below, 2010
pencil pen and acyrlic on paper
6 x 7.75 inches

Bottom Right:
Little Ladder, 2010
pencil pen and acyrlic on paper
7.75 x 6 inches

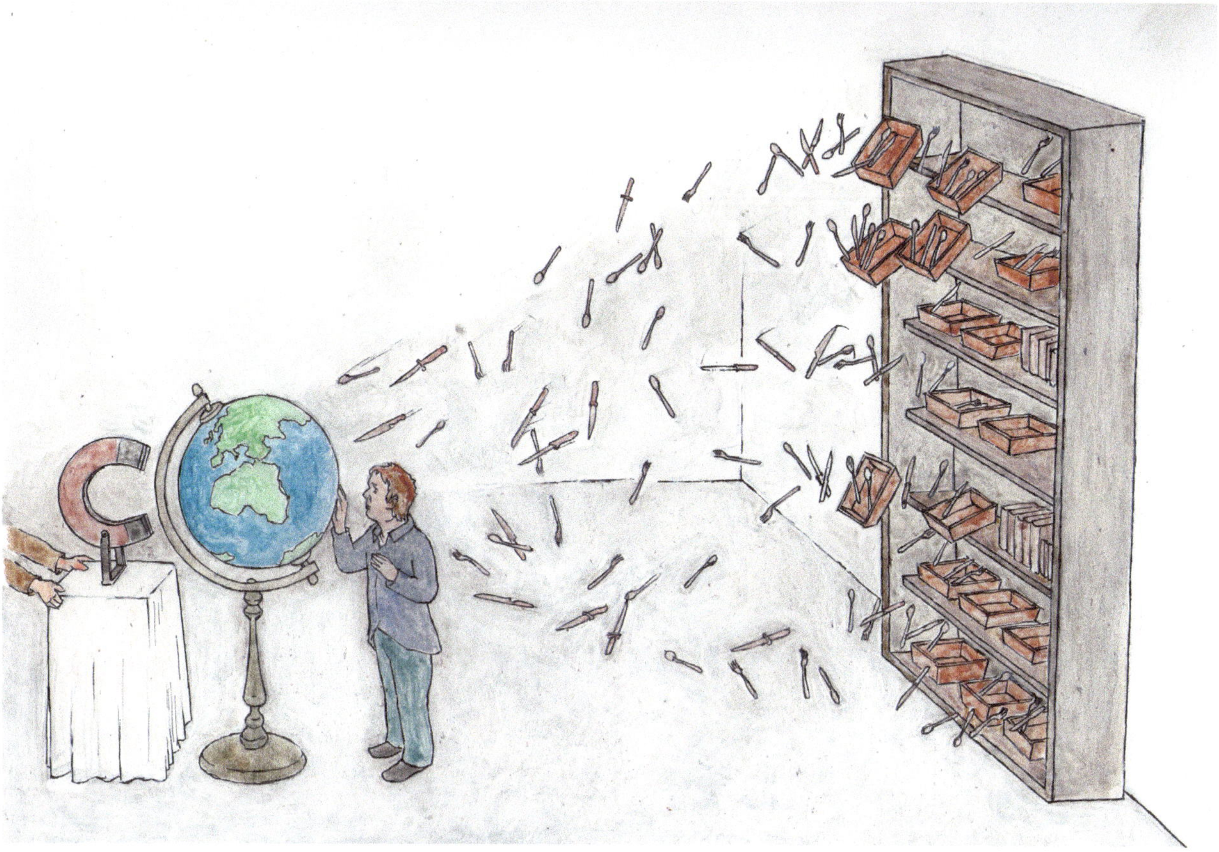

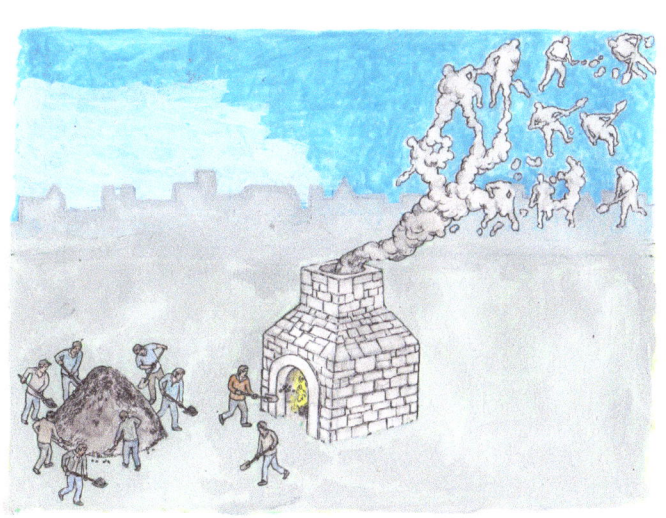

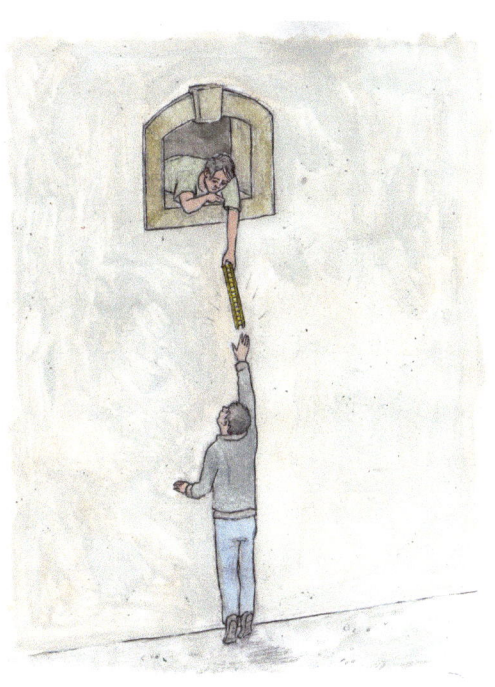

Lesley Guy

Sheffield, England

STATEMENT:

The recent project 'Obituaries' came from an attempt to use found, and random images as a strategy for image making. My original concern was with exploring ideas of loss by collecting, and archiving the obituary pages from the newspaper. I was fascinated with the way that those who were recently deceased had become transformed into images of paper and ink, their lives reduced to a few paragraphs. The project was compulsive but the strategy gradually evolved into exploring the surface of the photographic images; within the process is a struggle between contingency and control. Here I use drawing as a tool for thinking and exploring; I enjoy solving the problems of surface, picture plane, illusion and form.

I am often drawn to an image for some visual or compositional aspect, for example, those wearing spectacles might be chosen, sometimes those with two people looking at each other, sometimes if the background is blurred or if the hand bears an interesting relation to the face. I then work to enhance these characteristics often using continuous lines to build up forms and veils.

There are over 100 drawings in the archive and there are as many different categories into which they can be sorted and displayed. The personal histories of the people have some meaning, but this is often superficial, focusing occasionally on the profession, age or gender of the deceased. The meticulous defacement and transformation of the image into a formal game of composition is the subject rather than the biography.

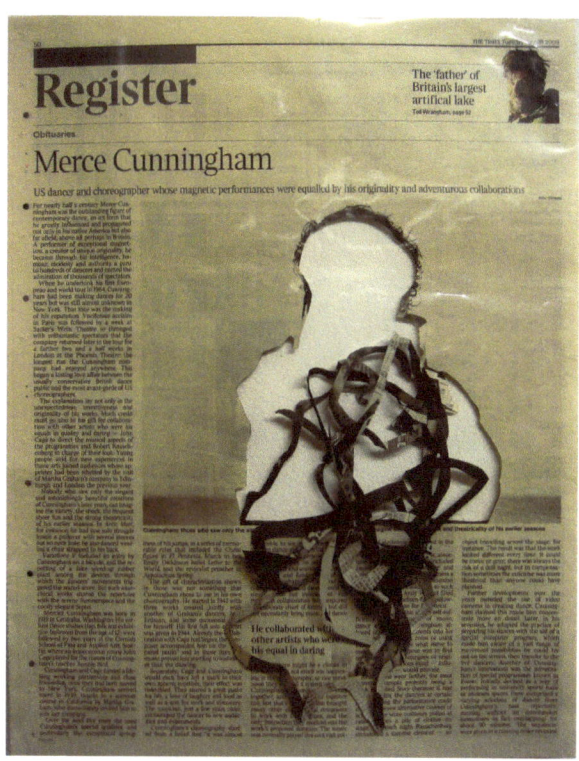

Top:
Cunningham, 2012
Acrylic paint on newspaper
Dimensions variable

Bottom:
Metamorphosis, 2012
Acrylic paint on newspaper
Dimensions variable

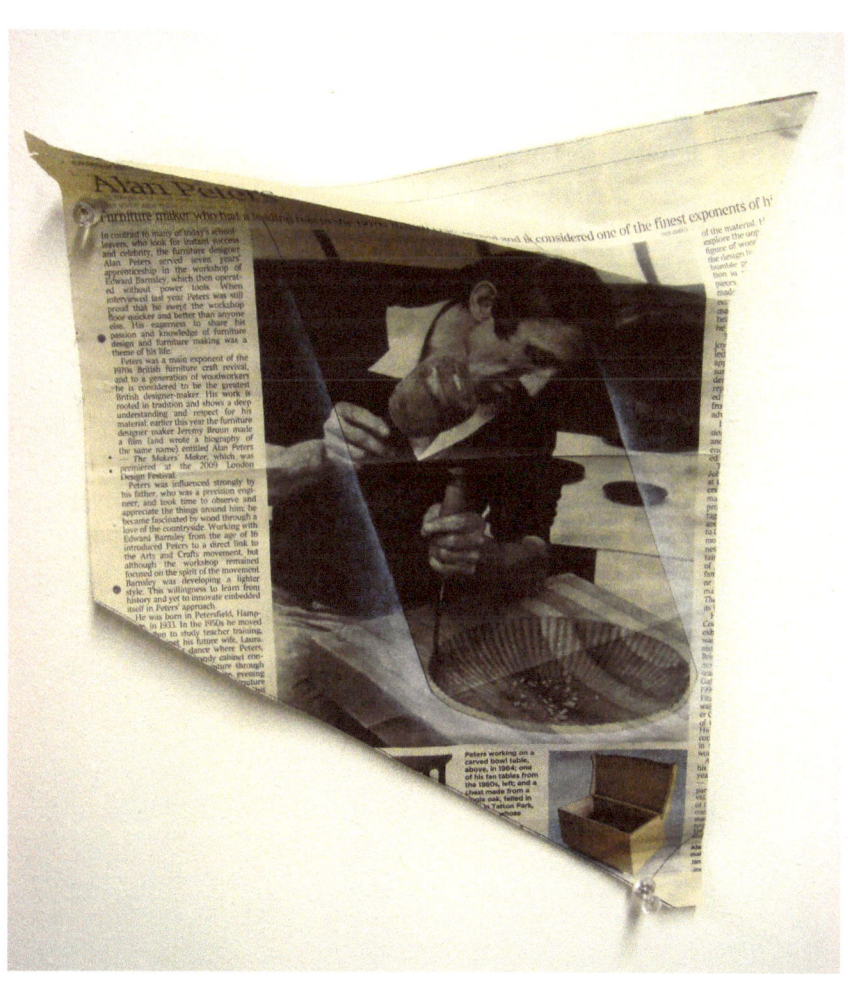

Mark Keffer

Cleveland, Ohio, USA

STATEMENT:

My work is intended to echo the fragmentary, open-ended nature of thinking and to create a visual reality that is simultaneously austere and hopeful — an honest reflection of my view of life. I try to construct a world of images and meanings that embrace the fringes of consciousness. I want to empty the work of subjects that are primarily verbal in nature to directly access aspects of beauty, imagination and the vast, indeterminate realm of human thought and emotion.

There is an existential mindset at work — a philosophy of no philosophy — guided by a bent toward the ridiculous. The work contains symbols for the unknowable and hints of the far reaches of outer space which serve as wry metaphors for the occupations of the mind.

ABOUT:

Mark Keffer was born and raised in Cleveland, Ohio, USA. He received a BFA degree from Kent State University (1988) and an MFA from Ohio State University (1991). He lived, worked and exhibited in New York City from 1996-2005. Teaching positions have included Kent State and Youngstown State Universities. Currently residing in Cleveland, his work has been exhibited extensively on the regional level; it has also been shown nationally and internationally. Solo exhibitions have been held in Cleveland, Youngstown, and Athens, Ohio; Phoenix, Arizona; Greenwich, Connecticut and NYC. Residency programs include The Millay Colony for the Arts, Ucross Foundation and The Vermont Studio Center. He is a recipient of the Ohio Arts Council Individual Artist Fellowship.

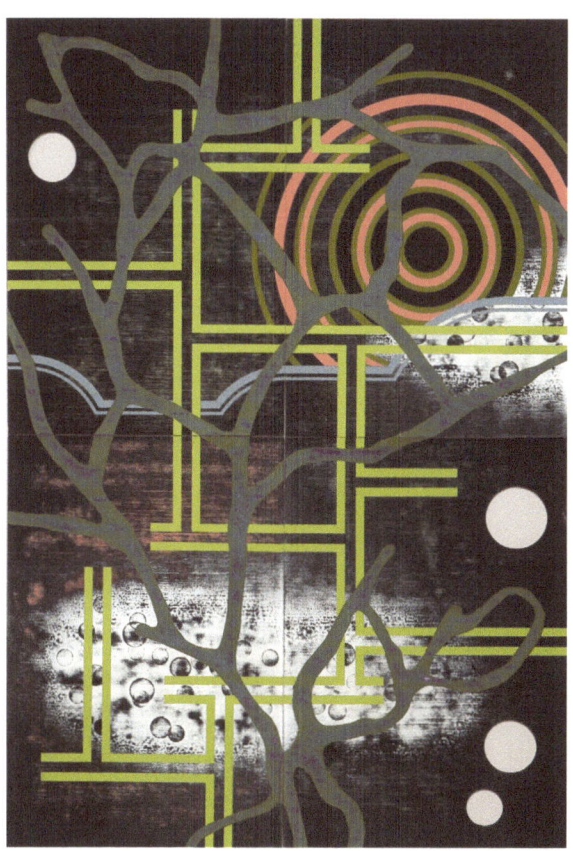

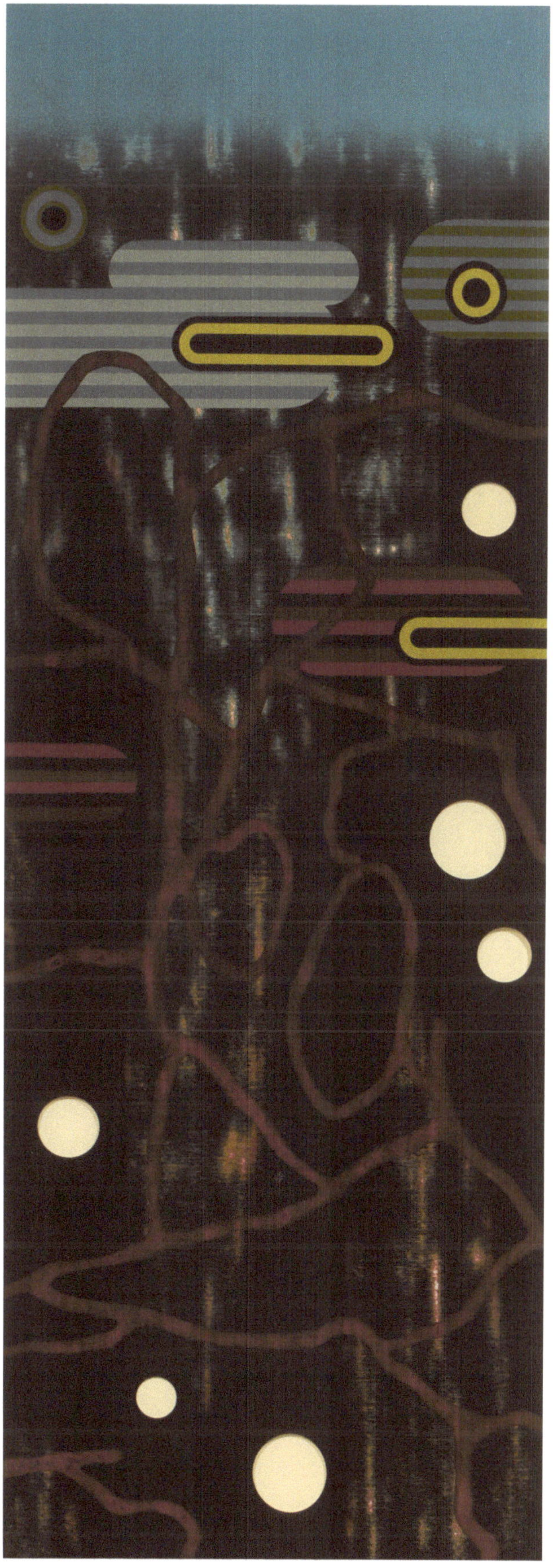

Left:
Unlikely Sun, 2012
acrylic and spray paint on cut paper,
four panels, 35 x 24"

Right:
Bright Blue Sky, 2012
acrylic and spray paint on cut paper,
two panels, 58 x 22"

Robert Lang

Bristol, England

STATEMENT:

Painting allows me to understand my relationship with certain decisions and judgements through a very tactile engagement with representation. These decisions follow an interest in the problems of perceived reality, underlying ideologies and cultural fictions that direct and sway our everyday experiences.

Reference material is usually hoarded from the internet reinforcing a sense of remote observation. These references usually allude to a shift in the way something can be perceived or experienced, whether in solice or as part of a tribal, national, or religious group.

My painting style is intentionally economical and figurative details are replaced with modulations in the surface, textures, thin glazed layers and tentative daubs. There is always a balance of the paintings' material form against/with its representational function, whether figurative or abstract. In the faltering transcription of these details, the paintings create an anarchic space, disregarding the need to establish certain ends but demanding engagement from the interpreter

ABOUT:

Robert Lang works in Newport & Bristol where he studied an MA at UWE Bristol (2005-8). Recent Exhibitions include Angelika Open, Angelika studios, High Wycombe (2012); Maarten van den Bos, Jaap de Vries, Robert Lang, Appels Gallery, Amsterdam (2012); Remote Viewing, Motorcade/Flashparade, Bristol (2011); Deptford X Open, Core Gallery, London (2011); Fade Away, Transition Gallery, London (2010); Salon, Matt Roberts, London (2010); Exeter Contemporary Open, Exeter Contemporary, Exeter (2010).

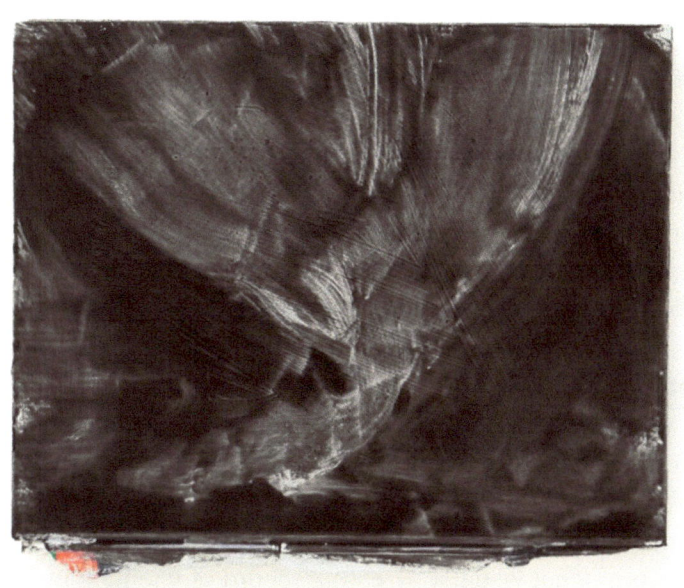

The North no. 2, 2012
Oil, book cover, birch plywood,
8.5 x 11 inches

Krystel Marois

Berlin, Germany

STATEMENT:

Portraiture and a focus on the human presence make up the vast majority of Marois' portfolio. These photographs often act as a deconstructive narrative of temporal human experience, allowing the viewer to draw their own conclusions of the depicted visual imagery as demonstrated by her series Sans Titre. As she enters the confined breathing spaces of her subject, she explores the boundaries between interior and exterior narratives while simultaneously blurring the lines between the two, often revealing personal characteristics of strength, vulnerability and isolation. Dynamic and teeming with intensity, her portraits seek to extract a singular raw, visceral moment of human emotion resulting in evocative yet sober representations of her subjects. This in turn allows the viewer to experience a liberating moment of truth about her protagonist, an important aspect for Marois' personal artistic motivations. However, the play between factual reality and the fictitious construction of the image create an ever-evolving dialogue between the viewer and the subject in the portrait. Ultimately, her figures are left with their private thoughts and interior turmoil; however the artist's portraits provide a visually arresting record of events which leave the viewer to ponder their own private narrative.

ABOUT:

Krystel Marois is a photographer originally from Sherbrooke (Canada) who lives and works in Berlin (Germany). She completed with honors a Bachelor of Fine Arts at Concordia University (Montreal, Canada) in 2010, with a major in Photography. She is interested in contemporary portraiture, as well as traces of human presence in landscapes and interiors through which she depicts a deconstructed narrative with a cinematic aesthetic. Her photographs have mostly been shown in Canada and in Europe and are part of private collections.

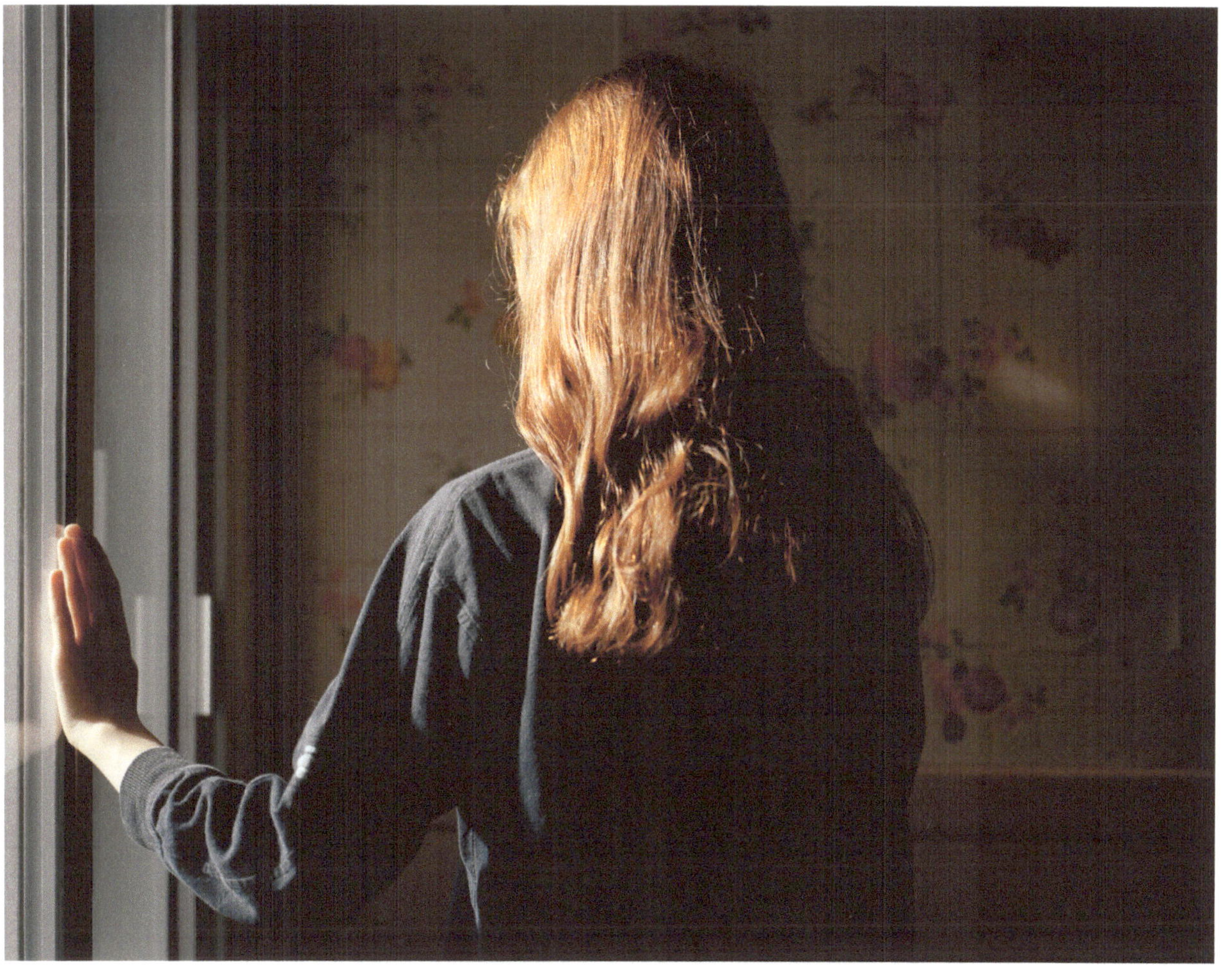

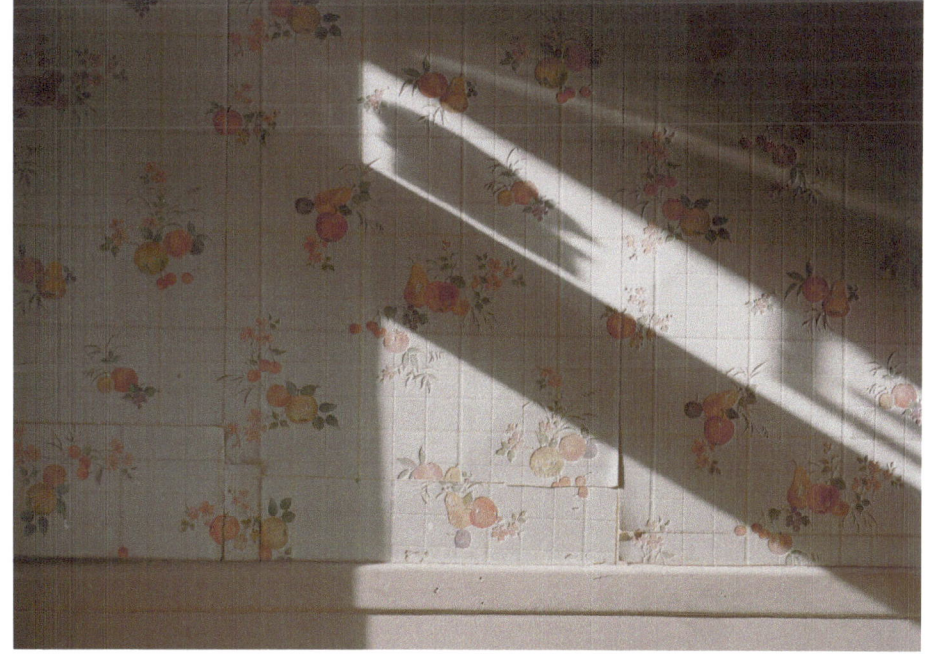

Top:
Red Hair, 2010
c-print, Edition of 7
30 x 40"

Bottom:
Afternoon Sun, 2010
c-print, Edition of 7
30 x 40"

Jonathan McFadden

Minnesota, USA

STATEMENT:

My work explores the cacophony of imagery in news cycles and how the presentation of this imagery has deferred an understanding of the information and the landscapes it presents. The bombardment of information associated with contemporary media outlets creates a culture and atmosphere of urgency that intensely focuses on the present. The often haste and theatric nature of new cycles does not allow for proper reflection and analysis of events.

Instead the narrative of media events blur into one another regardless of their relationship to one another. As a global society is presented with these fragmented narratives it is left with a lack of linear narrative that promotes a lack of memory.

News cycles become a catalyst in my prints and installations. By appropriating digital imagery and geographic information from news events I create a catalog of deconstructed imagery that through digital and traditional print matrixes is layered in reaction to these events. The imagery that is used to often dramatize events for entertainment becomes decorative pattern in my work.

In these works I seek to address the dystopic global narrative that is presented by media outlets. The reaction to a culture of ephemeral narratives presented by the fast pace of information creates the jumbled and densely layered imagery in my work.

ABOUT:

Jonathan McFadden holds a MFA in printmaking from Edinburgh College of Art, BFA in Printmaking, and BA in French from Texas State University. His work has been exhibited at the National Gallery of Scotland, Royal Scottish Academy, University of Texas- San Antonio, University of Wisconsin- Madison, the University of Minnesota, Millsaps College and many other national and international venues. Jonathan has taught at Minnesota State University- Mankato, Houston Community College, and Edinburgh College of Art and is currently Assistant Professor of Printmaking at Minnesota State University- Mankato.

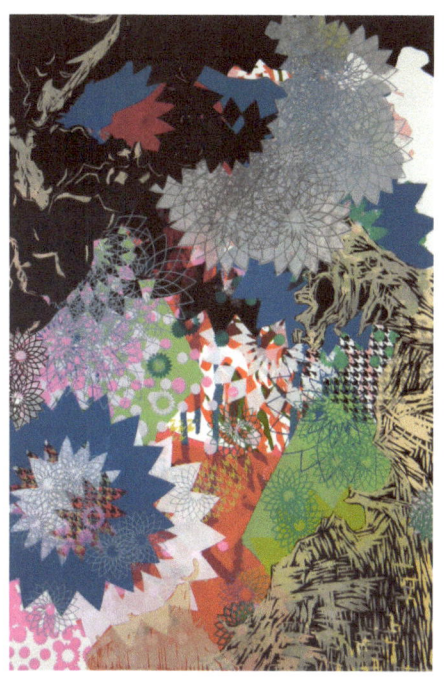

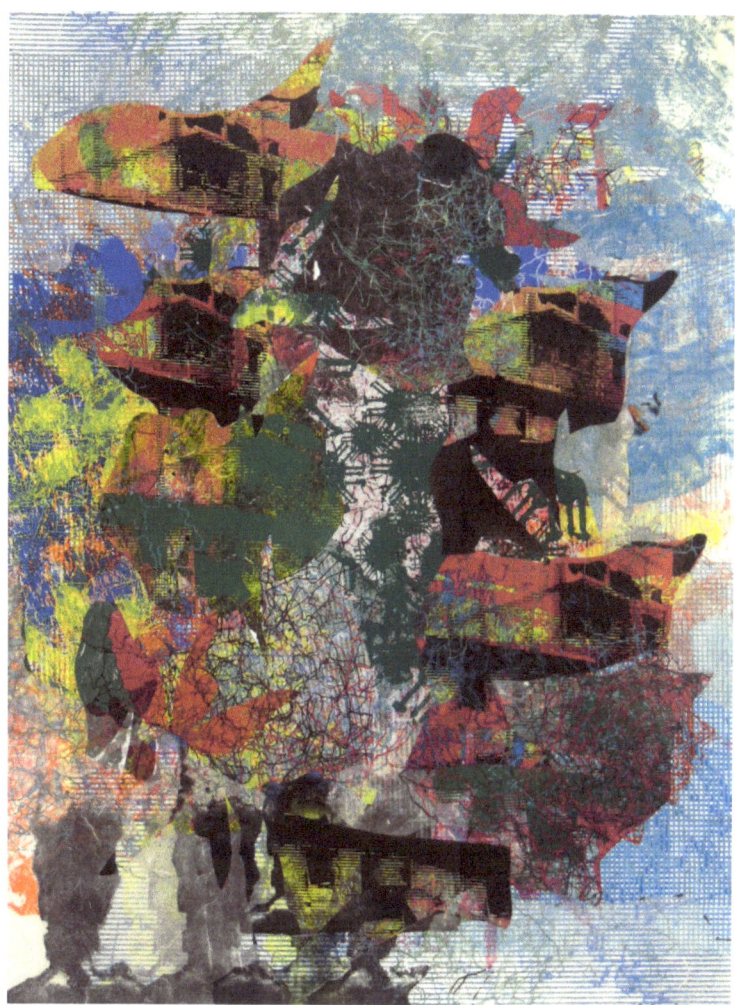

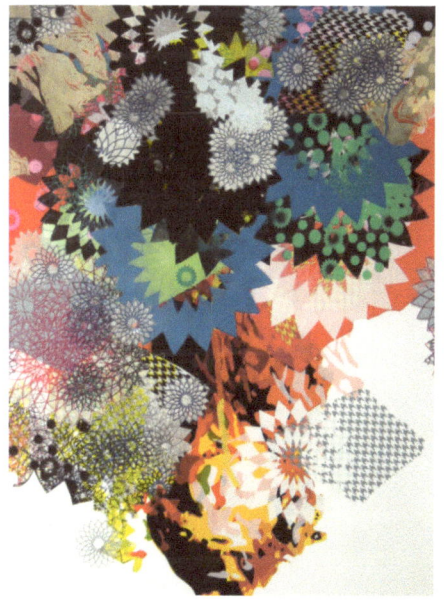

Top Left:
Suing Other Companies For Accountability, 2011
Screen and Relief Print With Chine-colle
22" x 15"

Right:
Expelling Diplomats, 2012
Screen Print and Chine-Colle
24" x 18"

Bottom:
66 Kilometers, 2011
Screen and Relief print on digital print
with chine-colle, 24" x 18"

Haroob Mullick

London, England

STATEMENT:

My work practice at the present:
To create a practice, I give myself a template or formula or perhaps an exercise to achieve a flow in mark making. Currently this is done by only working in black and white, and its subsequent grays. By not introducing colours and limiting each series to 12 to 24, it gives me the constraint or framework to be able to create freely.

The work is based in a form of a personal narrative with the sub conscious; the method of work begins with a choice of a series of numbers. This numerical approach enables the event of drawing to commence. It is a struggle between constraint and freedom as the subconscious element of the process can be at times overwhelming.

The final pieces reflect a personal mythology which have recurring symbols, patterns and narratives. This, I associate or disassociate at a time of viewing.

So predominately at the present I am still working toward the flow between the seated subconsciousness and with the form of the materials I use as means of expression.

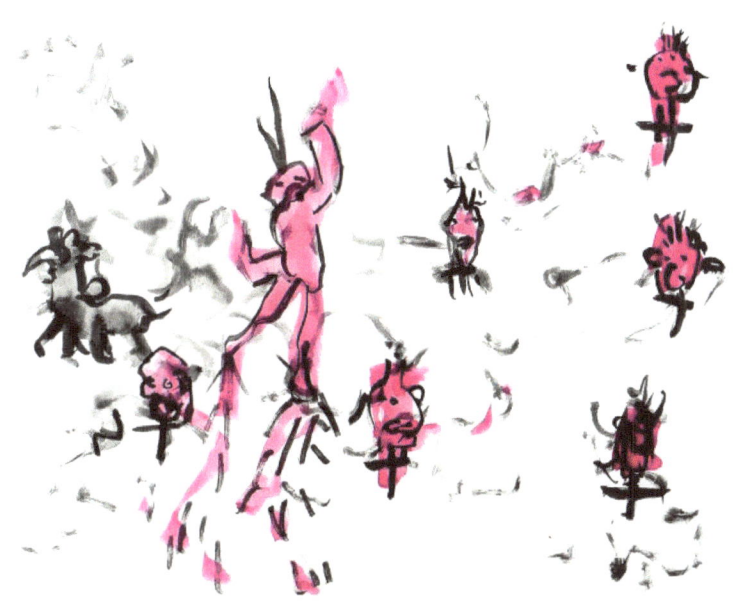

parisB, 2012
japanese ink and graphite stick on paper

Lydia Panas

Pennsylvania, USA

STATEMENT:

Making a photograph allows me to stare, describe and represent an interaction. I make pictures about expectations and about the uncertainty in relationships.

Falling from Grace... is a series of portraits that speaks to issues of connections and trust. Despite a forthright appearance these faces suggest a tension. We are not sure how to receive their expressions. The faces are vague and uncommitted. It is not clear if the models offer or withhold. These portraits connect and disengage simultaneously, proposing a precarious intimacy.

ABOUT:

Lydia Panas's Fine Art photography has been exhibited internationally and is held in major public collections including the Brooklyn Museum, the Museum of Fine arts Houston, the Museum of Contemporary Photography, Chicago., and MoMA Shanghai.

Lydia's work has been represented extensively in publications such as the New York Times Magazine, Photo District News, Popular Photography, and the Wall Street Journal Blog..

Lydia has degrees from Boston College, the School of Visual Arts and New York University / International Center of Photography as well as a Whitney Museum Independent Study Fellowship.

Her first monograph The Mark of Abel was released by Kehrer Verlag and named one of Photo District News "Best Books of 2012".

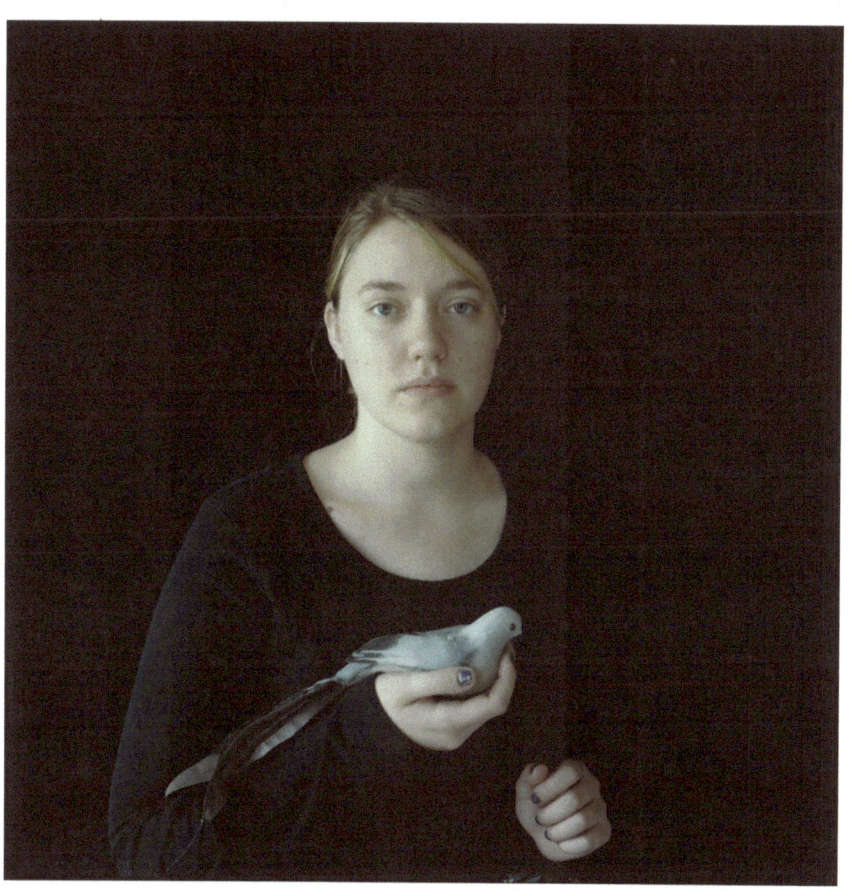

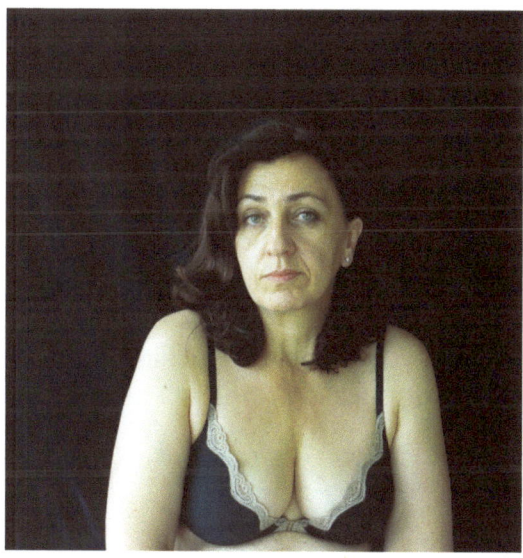

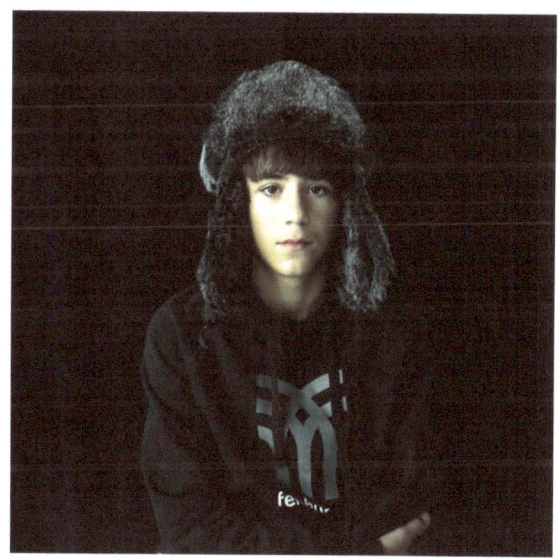

Top:
Bird
Photograph on vinyl
from the "Falling from Grace" series
30 x 30 inches

Bottom Left:
Bra
Photograph on vinyl
from the "Fur and Skin" series
30 x 30 inches

Bottom Right:
Fur
Photograph on vinyl
from the "Fur and Skin" series
30 x 30 inches

Julia Schmid

Berlin, Germany

STATEMENT:

My art develops from books and time in a time that the actual book is in danger of extinction and time is considered to be a very rare good.

The rapidly and steadily increasing flow of information and collective knowledge in a more and more advancing, overstrained, overworked but still functioning society and the turn of written language to picture language through Internet, television and smartphones bother me.

How does this affect our thinking and communication?

My crucial question is: How much do we really know and how much do we pretend to know?

Whilst working on one of my pieces I engage myself intensively with Literature, philosophy and history. I leave the information in disguise, though, wishing to evoke new questions, thoughts and notions.

ABOUT:

Julia Schmid, Born in 1980, dedicated her interests and ability completely to the medium of letter drawings and does this on the one hand side with an almost manic and stoic calmness as on the other with a big trust in the spontaneous and fast end-to-end lines. She creates ink drawings, that are based on written words within which her oeuvre became a kind of collective unawareness of philosophical texts and music. The exhibited "Fingertanz" is one piece of a multiparted ongoing series. Each drawing is a kind of individual characterization of a certain song from different cultures.

Chris Bierl – Nov. 2012

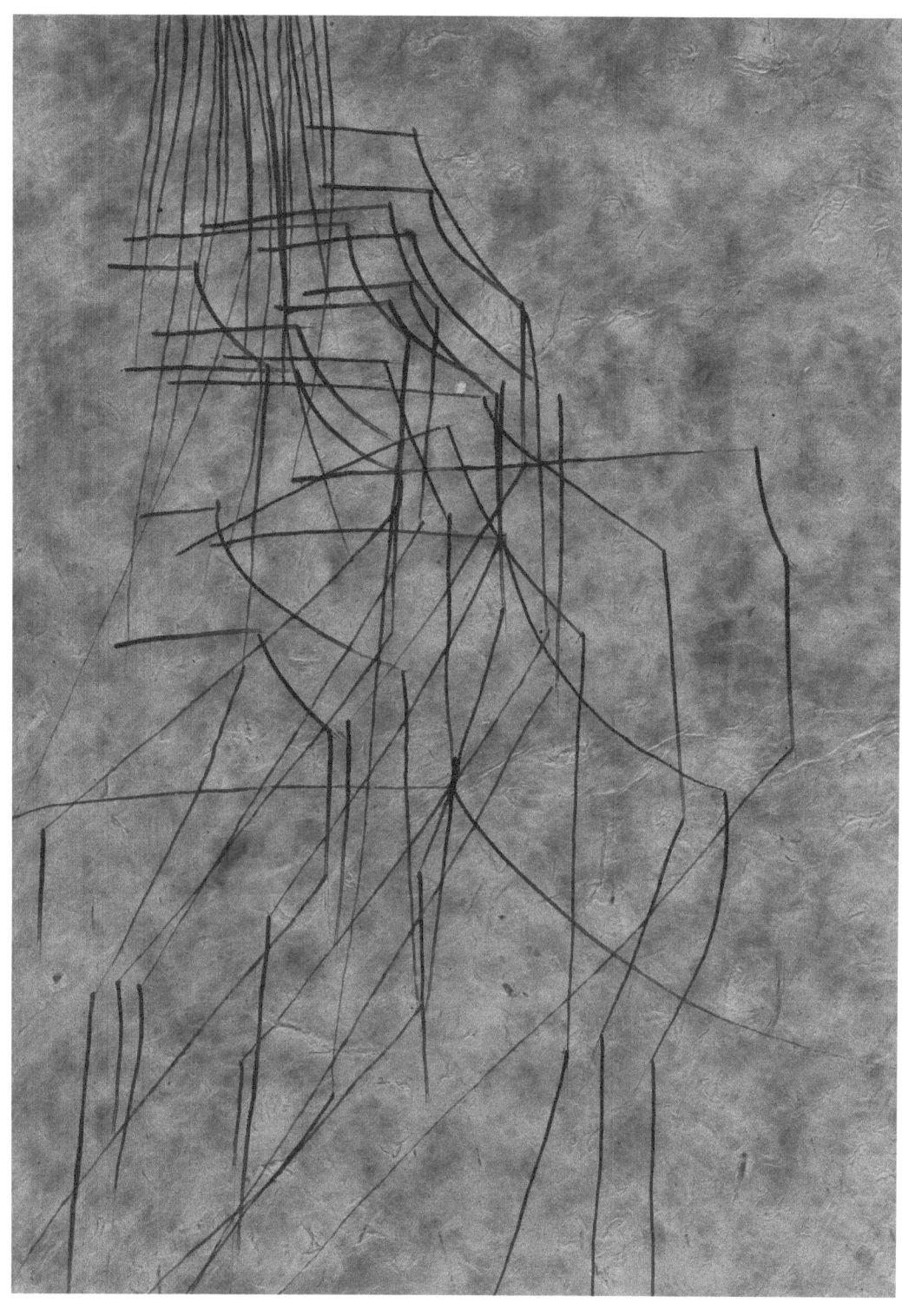

Untitled, ("Fingertänze" series), 2012
Ink on paper
15.75 x 11.5 inches

Mercedes Teixido

California, USA

STATEMENT:

Writing is drawing and drawing is writing.

These images are inspired by poetry, signage, and the material presence of form. They are rooted in the notion of improvisation; these drawings are performed into existence. An invented alphabet, the total collection of images becoming an image sentence of sorts. The familiar is laminated to the unfamiliar, and language in all its forms, is continually reinvented.

ABOUT:

Born in Wilmington, Delaware part of a large family from Paraguay. Educated at Wake Forest University in North Carolina and at the University of Arizona. Work includes explorations on paper, letter writing and art pieces made for individuals and their domestic settings.

Mercedes teaches in southern California at Pomona College and lives in the Catskills of New York in the summers.

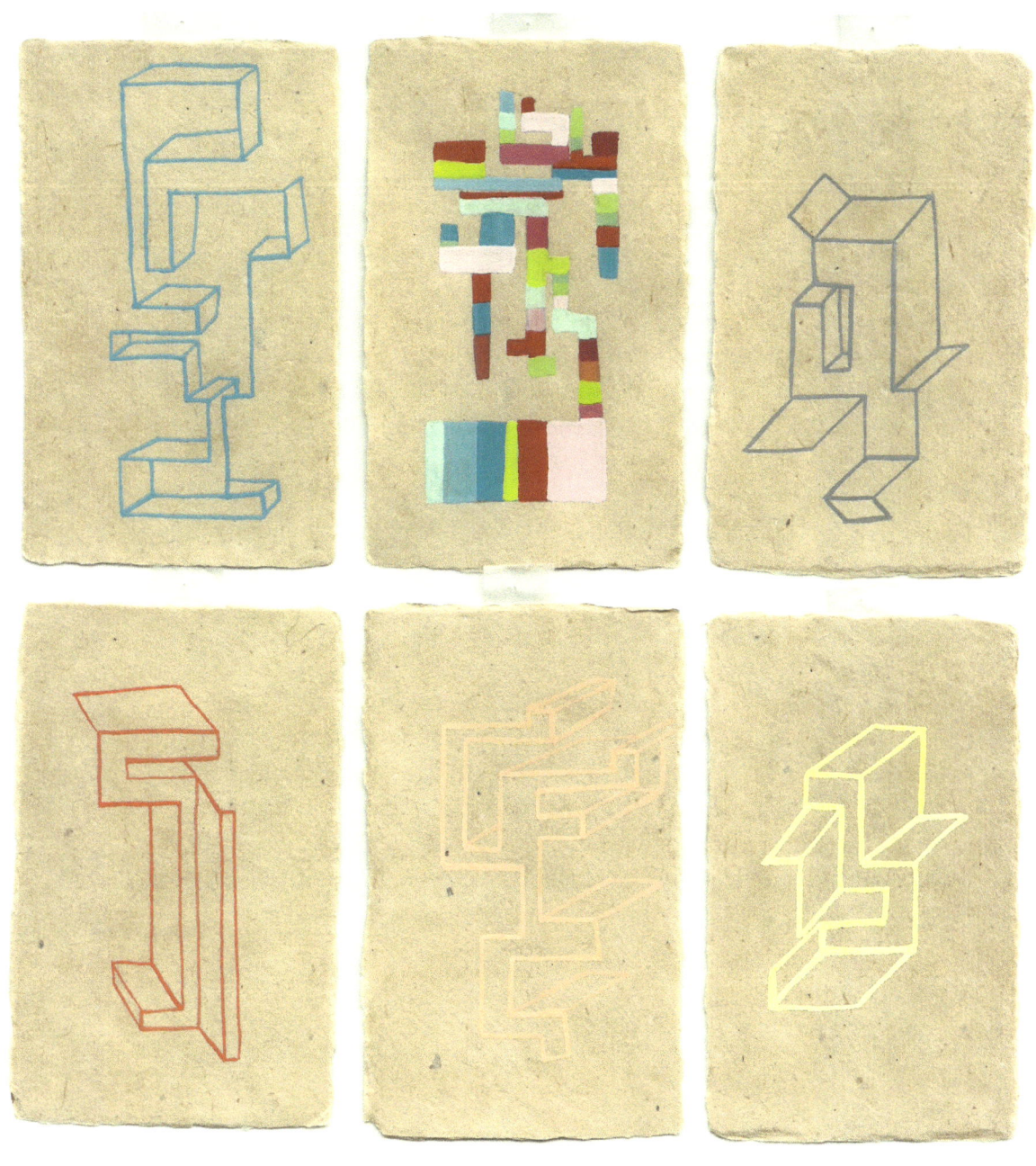

The Thread, 2011-2012
Watercolor on handmade paper
2" x 3.5" each, dimensions variable

Joshua Thomson

Hong Kong, China

STATEMENT:

"The Ultimate City" is the second instalment in a series of short films charting the 'achievements' of polymath Joshua WF Thomson. A critique of the cult of the artist-genius the film is also an attempt to project an alternative self, a person that can achieve the unachievable and realise the most audacious and eccentric of plans.

The films act as both wish fulfilment and parodies of myself and my artistic ambitions.

ABOUT:

British born Joshua Thomson is an award winning artist, musician and curator currently living and working in Hong Kong. Graduating from The Royal College of Art in 2003, Joshua Thomson has since exhibited widely in Europe, the USA and Asia. After working as the curator at the Fishmarket gallery in Northampton, U.K. Thomson moved to Asia in 2010 to establish the Platinum Metres label and concentrate on his artistic practice.

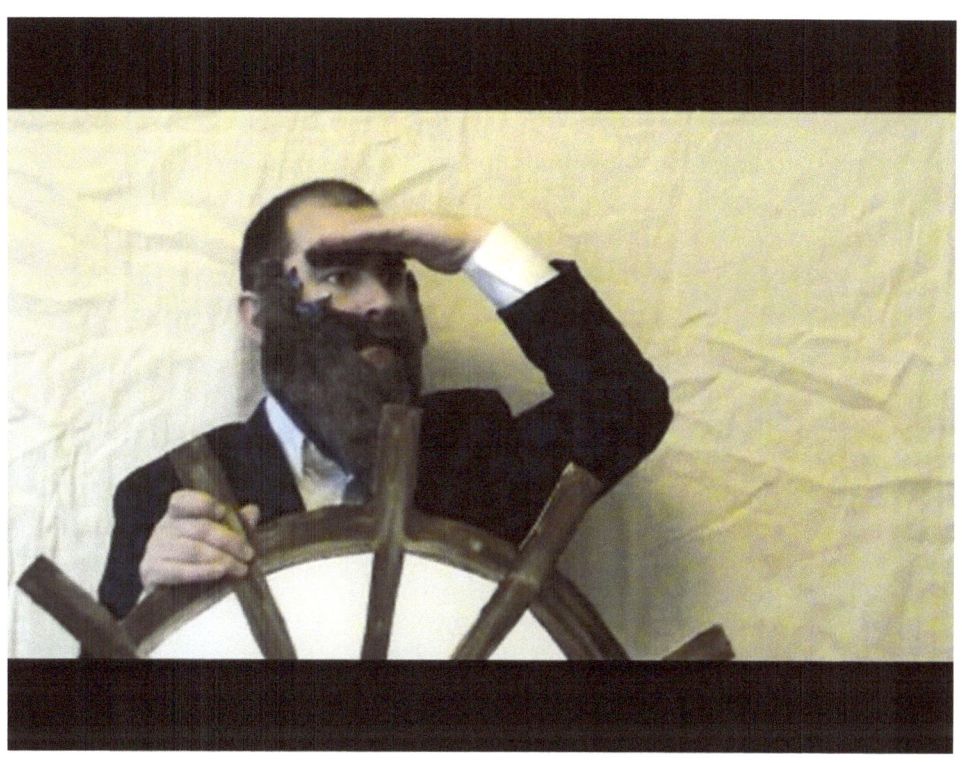

Still from: *The Ultimate City*, 2010
Digital video
6:51

Margaret Withers

New York City, New York, USA

STATEMENT:

"Painting the American Anti-Story" project is an ongoing body of work that strives to create in the viewer that liminal space between the point of recognition of an identifiable form and the abstract; I believe that in this space, creativity can creep in. My hope is that these anti-story paintings would reveal an illuminating narrative cut, as if a flash bulb pop across the space of an implied narrative, allowing for a pause in order to engage the viewer, to give them some time in this space- to figure out the story, or to pretend a new one. My art strives to engage the viewer in a creative collaboration; with each viewing, and with each viewer, layer upon layer of interpretation is added, and what someone else sees changes what someone else initially saw, and so on, to some point over time to where a new medium exist in the space between my art and the viewer.

ABOUT:

Margaret Withers was born in Austin, Texas in 1965. Her father worked in the oil industry and because of the nature of the work they moved frequently, Withers' dealt with this constant change by casting herself as both playwright and lead actor in countless fictions. She attended Texas A&M University where she received a BA in Literature. She moved to Colorado in 1991 and worked primarily in hand-built porcelain. In 1998 she started a series of mixed-media oil paintings with cast porcelain heads pushed into the canvas. In 2004 she attended CU Boulder's MFA program but did not matriculate, instead deciding to move to New York City in 2006. In 2011 she started working primarily on paper with watercolor, ink and enamel on overlapping series that explore migration, identity, belonging and the American anti-story. Her art has shown extensively in the US, and internationally in Europe, China and Moscow.

Top:
Fleeing Ike, 2011
Watercolor, ink and enamel on paper
30" x 22"

Bottom Left:
*Blushing Eastward Where
Blue Earth is Gathered*, 2012
watercolor, ink and enamel on paper
30"x22"

Bottom Right:
*Duchess Pyjama Cassowary Shyly
Moved Among the Leaves*, 2012
watercolor, ink, gouache and
enamel on paper
50"x30"

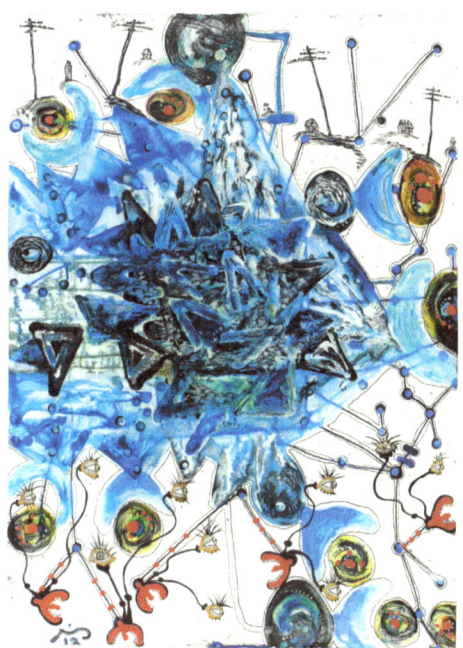

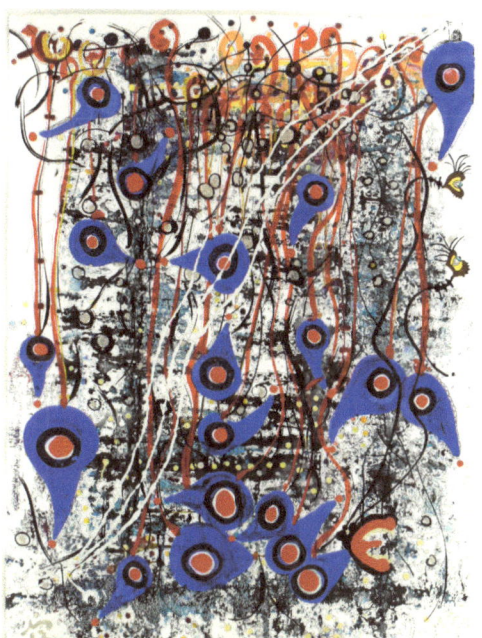

Das Wird Sich Alles Finden
[everything will turn out alright]